Pickup Lines

The Ultimate Collection of the World's Best Pickup Lines!

Table of Contents

Introduction

Thank you for picking up this book, full of hundreds of the best pickup lines!

Some of these lines are hilarious, some are corny, and some are downright dirty and NSFW!

While we can't guarantee that these lines will actually get you lucky, they should at the very least supply you and your friends with some light-hearted entertainment.

Have fun flicking through the hundreds of different pickup lines within the following pages and trying them out for yourself. Good luck!

Pickup Lines

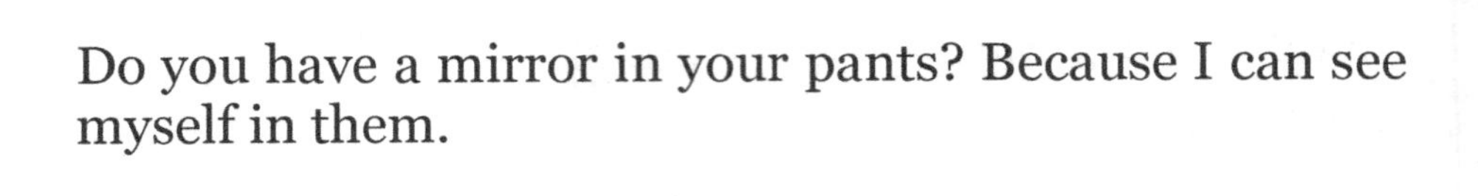

Do you have a mirror in your pants? Because I can see myself in them.

Do you know what my shirt is made out of? Boyfriend material.

I seem to have lost my phone number… could I borrow yours?

Are you a parking ticket? Because you've got FINE written all over you!

Is your dad a terrorist? Because you're the BOMB!

Kiss me if I'm wrong, but dinosaurs still exist, right?

Is your name Google? Because you're everything I've been searching for!

I may not be a genie, but I can make your wishes come true!

Are we in a museum? Because you're a work of art!

If you were words on a page, you'd be FINE print!

I was feeling a little bit off earlier, but you've turned me back on!

Anyone who says Disneyland is the happiest place on earth has clearly never stood next to you!

You're so hot, my zipper is falling for you!

They say the tongue is the strongest muscle in the body... Want to fight?

I'm always on top of things... would you like to be one of them?

Want to come over and watch some porn on my flat-screen mirror?

Is your name Winter? Because you'll be coming soon…

Are you an exam? Because I've been studying you non-stop!

Is your name Earl Grey? Because you look like a hot-tea!

I really love my bed, but I'd rather be in yours!

I really like your outfit! It would look amazing on my bedroom floor.

Is it hot in here? Or is it just you?

I've lost my keys. Can I check in your pants?

Are you an elevator? Because I'd go up and down on you.

Do you like raisins? How would you feel about a date?

What has 36 teeth and holds back the incredible hulk? My zipper.

Are you a cake? Because I want a piece of that!

Sorry, I'm new in town. Could you give me directions to your apartment?

If you were a potato, you'd be a sweet one.

People call me John, but you can call me tonight.

Do you like coffee? Because I like you a latte.

Well, here I am! Now what were your other two wishes?

Are you from Tennessee? Because you're the only Ten-I-See!

Do you know karate? Because your body is kickin'!

Are you a beaver? Because Daaaaaaaaaaaamn!

Is your name Rapunzel? Because I'm looking for a girl who never leaves the bedroom and constantly wants me to pull her hair!

Is your body from McDonalds? Because I'm lovin' it!

If you were a fruit, you'd be a fine-apple!

Did you swallow a magnet? Because you're attractive!

Wouldn't we look cute on a wedding cake together?

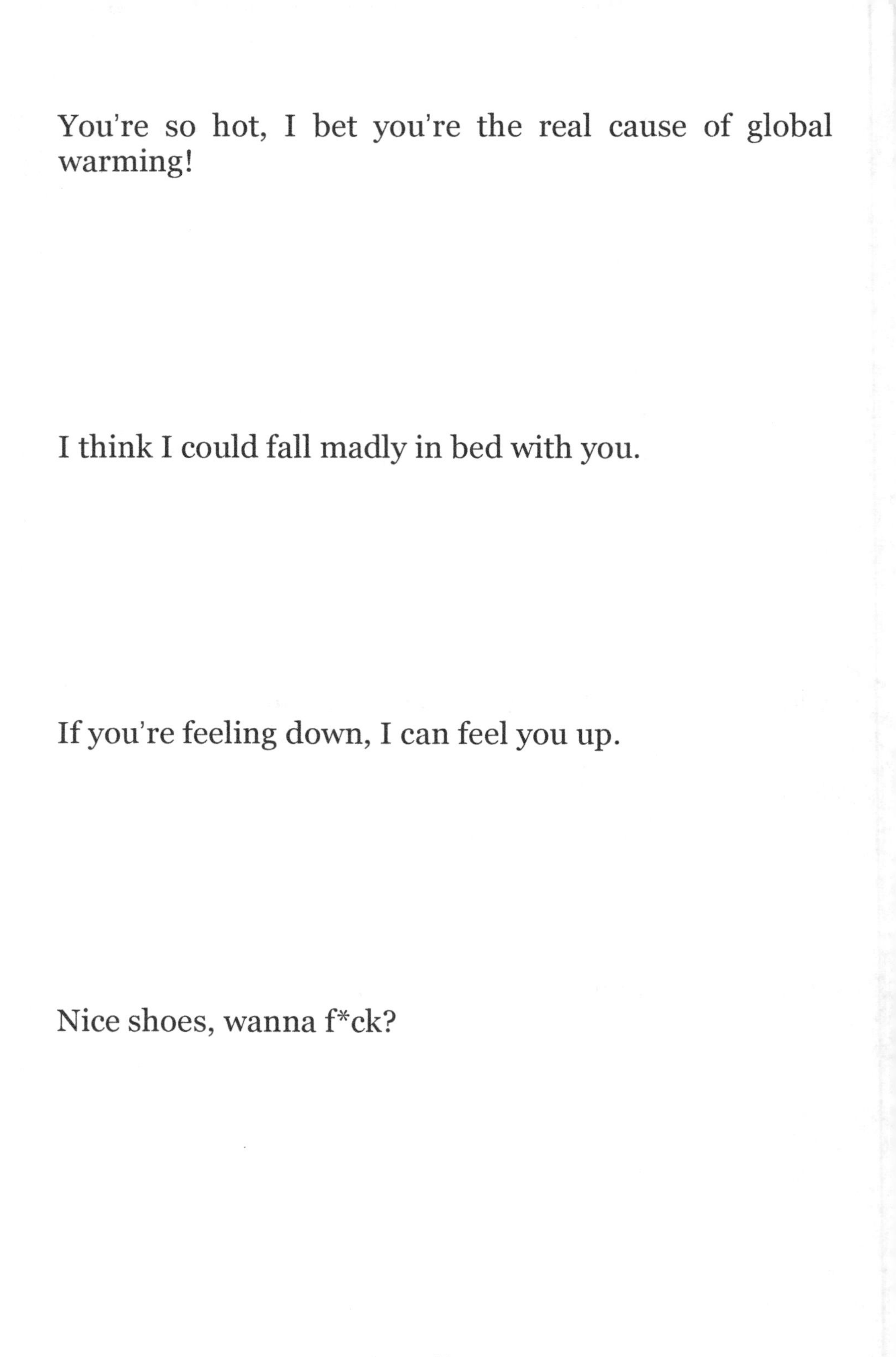

You're so hot, I bet you're the real cause of global warming!

I think I could fall madly in bed with you.

If you're feeling down, I can feel you up.

Nice shoes, wanna f*ck?

Let's play titanic. You play the iceberg, and I'll go down…

I really care about the environment. Want to save water by showering together?

Want to go halves on a baby?

Are you a sea lion? Because I can 'sea' you 'lion' in my bed tonight!

Hey, you dropped something. My jaw.

Call me Elmo, because you can tickle me whenever you want!

Nice dress, can I talk you out of it?

Is there a mirror in your pants? Because I can see myself in them!

Kiss me if I'm wrong, but isn't the earth flat?

Your hand looks heavy. Can I hold it for you?

I'd give up my morning cereal to spoon you instead!

Roses are red,

Violets are fine,

You be the 6,

And I'll be the 9!

That's a nice shirt! Can I try it on after we have sex?

Are you a drill sergeant? Because my privates are standing at attention!

If you were a flower, you'd be a damn-delion!

One a scale of 1-10, you're a 9. And I'm the 1 you need!

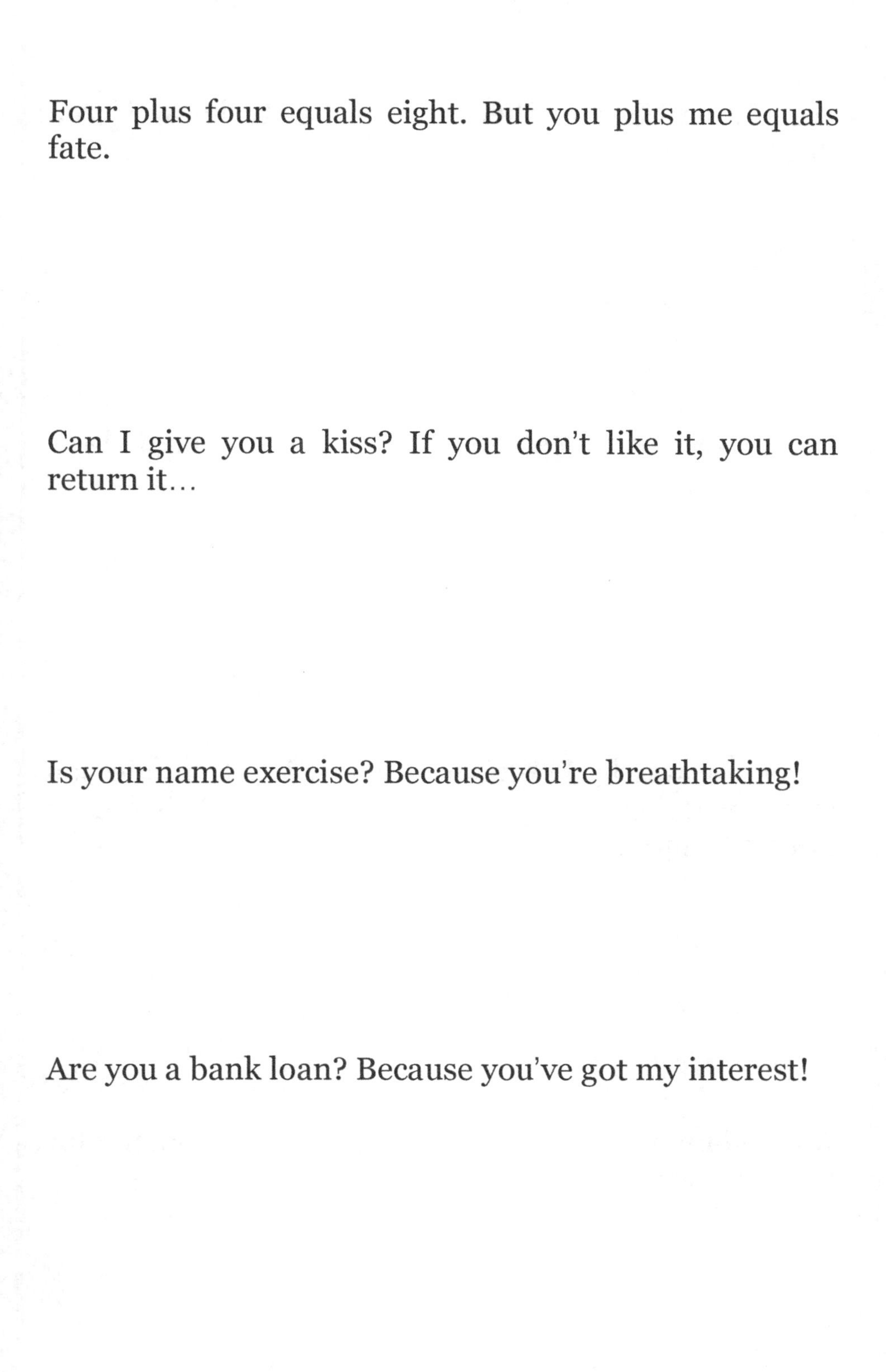

Four plus four equals eight. But you plus me equals fate.

Can I give you a kiss? If you don't like it, you can return it…

Is your name exercise? Because you're breathtaking!

Are you a bank loan? Because you've got my interest!

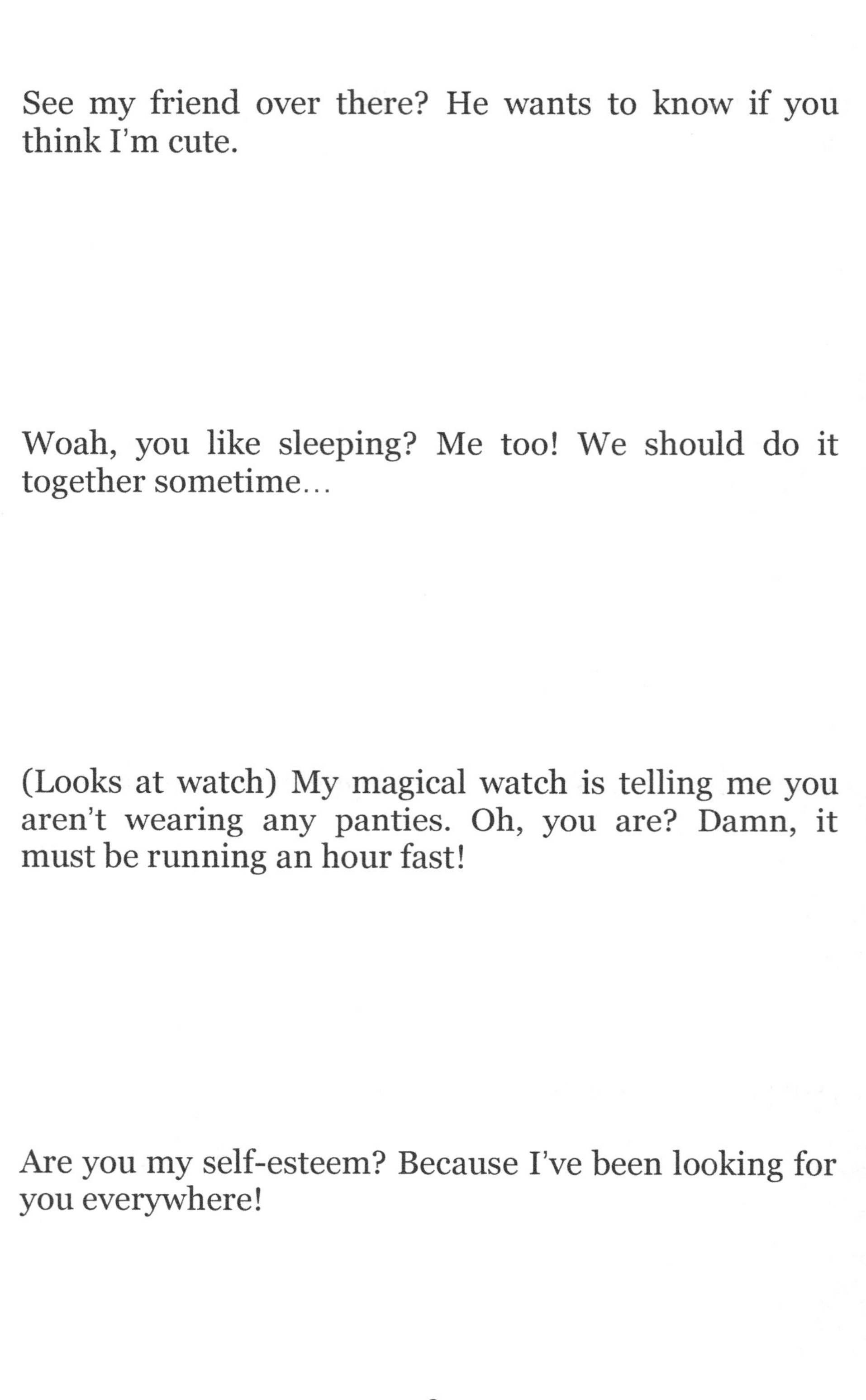

See my friend over there? He wants to know if you think I'm cute.

Woah, you like sleeping? Me too! We should do it together sometime…

(Looks at watch) My magical watch is telling me you aren't wearing any panties. Oh, you are? Damn, it must be running an hour fast!

Are you my self-esteem? Because I've been looking for you everywhere!

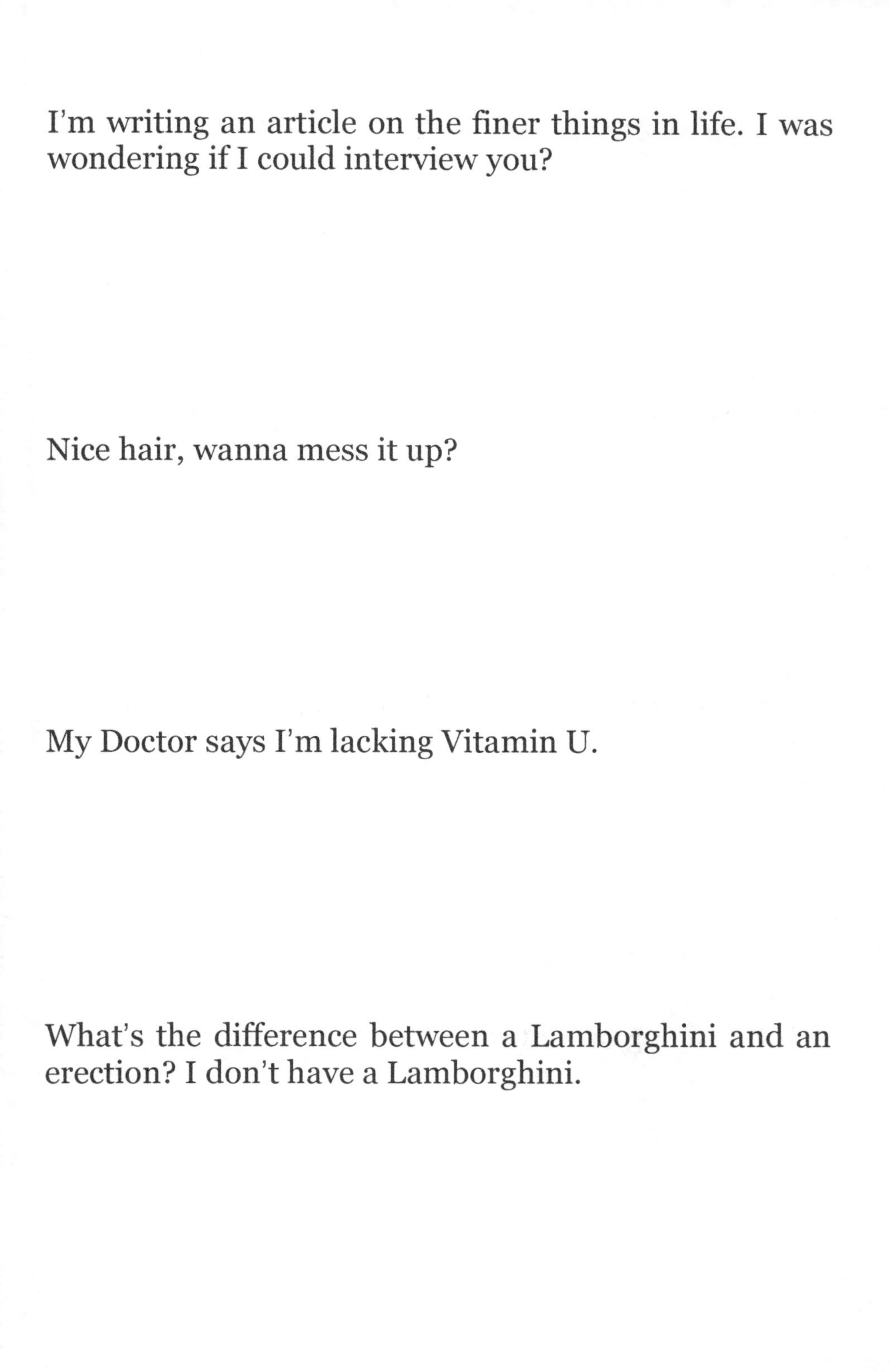

I'm writing an article on the finer things in life. I was wondering if I could interview you?

Nice hair, wanna mess it up?

My Doctor says I'm lacking Vitamin U.

What's the difference between a Lamborghini and an erection? I don't have a Lamborghini.

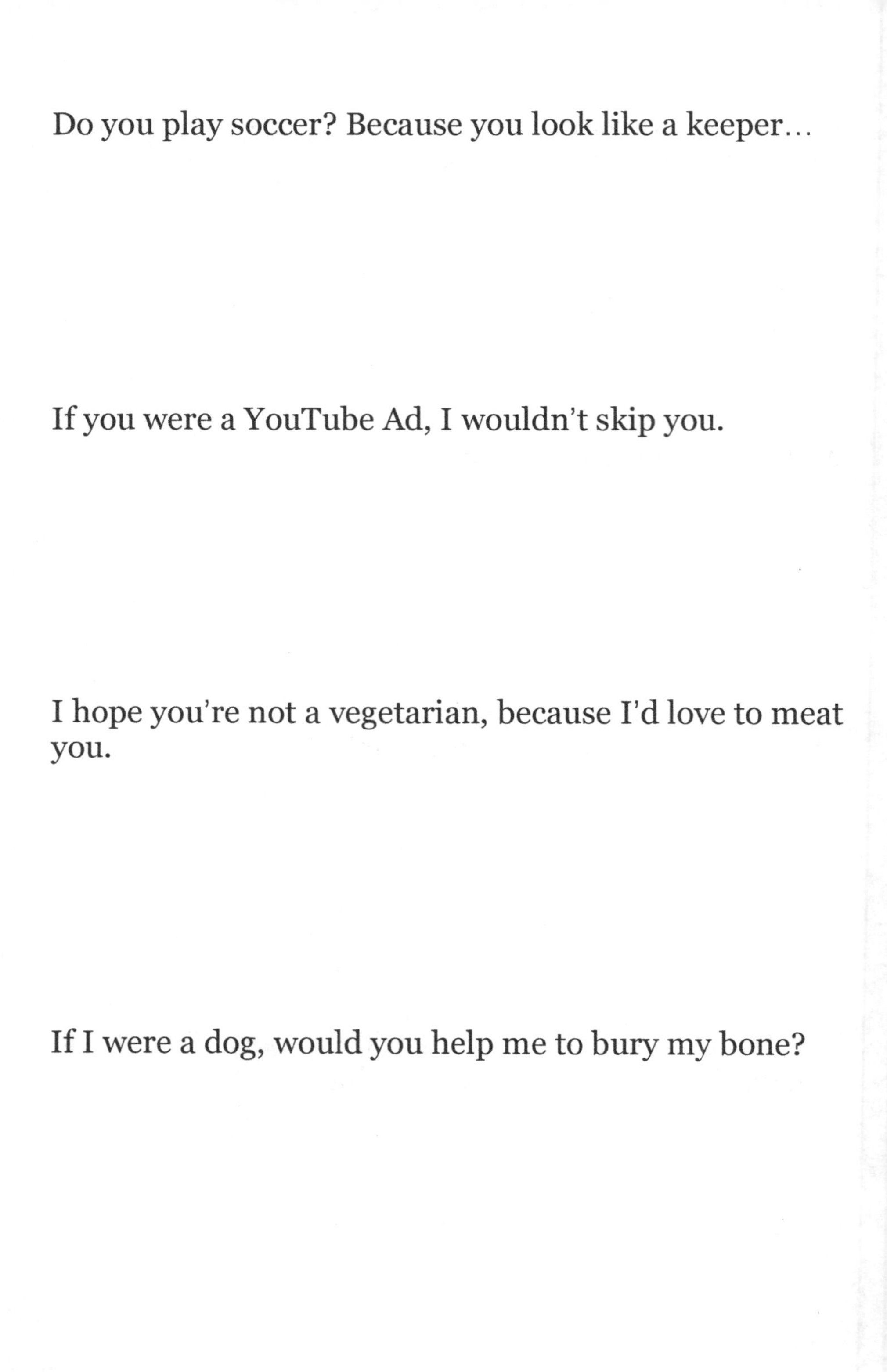

Do you play soccer? Because you look like a keeper…

If you were a YouTube Ad, I wouldn't skip you.

I hope you're not a vegetarian, because I'd love to meat you.

If I were a dog, would you help me to bury my bone?

Is your name Daniel? Because DAMN!

Damn girl, are you my appendix? Because I can't figure out how you work, but this feeling in my stomach makes me want to take you out!

I put the STD in STUD. All I need is U.

I lost my teddy bear. Will you sleep with me instead?

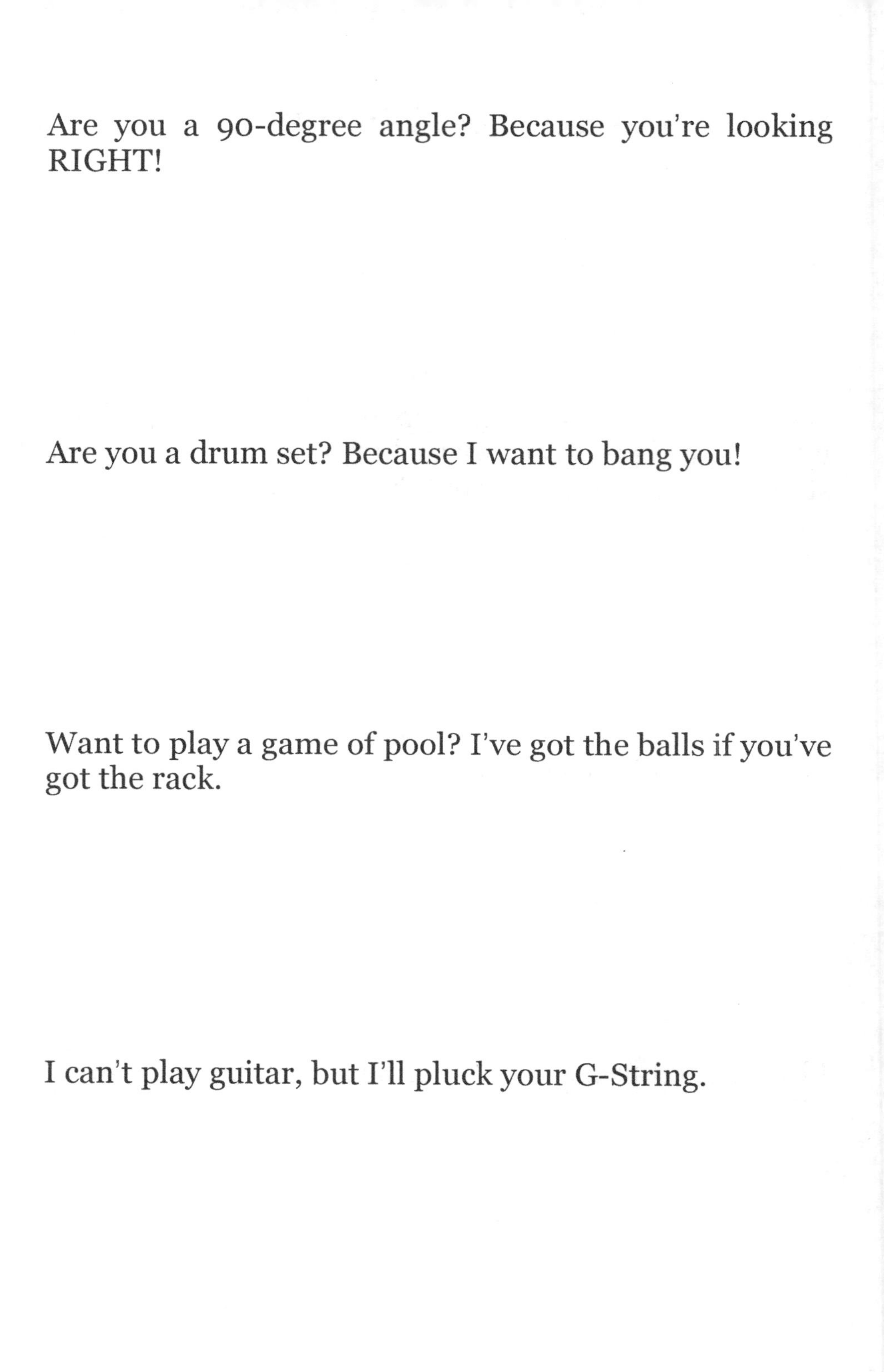

Are you a 90-degree angle? Because you're looking RIGHT!

Are you a drum set? Because I want to bang you!

Want to play a game of pool? I've got the balls if you've got the rack.

I can't play guitar, but I'll pluck your G-String.

Do you believe in love at first sight? Or should I walk by again?

Is your name Cinderella? Because I can see that dress disappearing at midnight…

Did you know the human body has 206 bones in it? Want another?

Can I borrow a kiss? I promise I'll give it back!

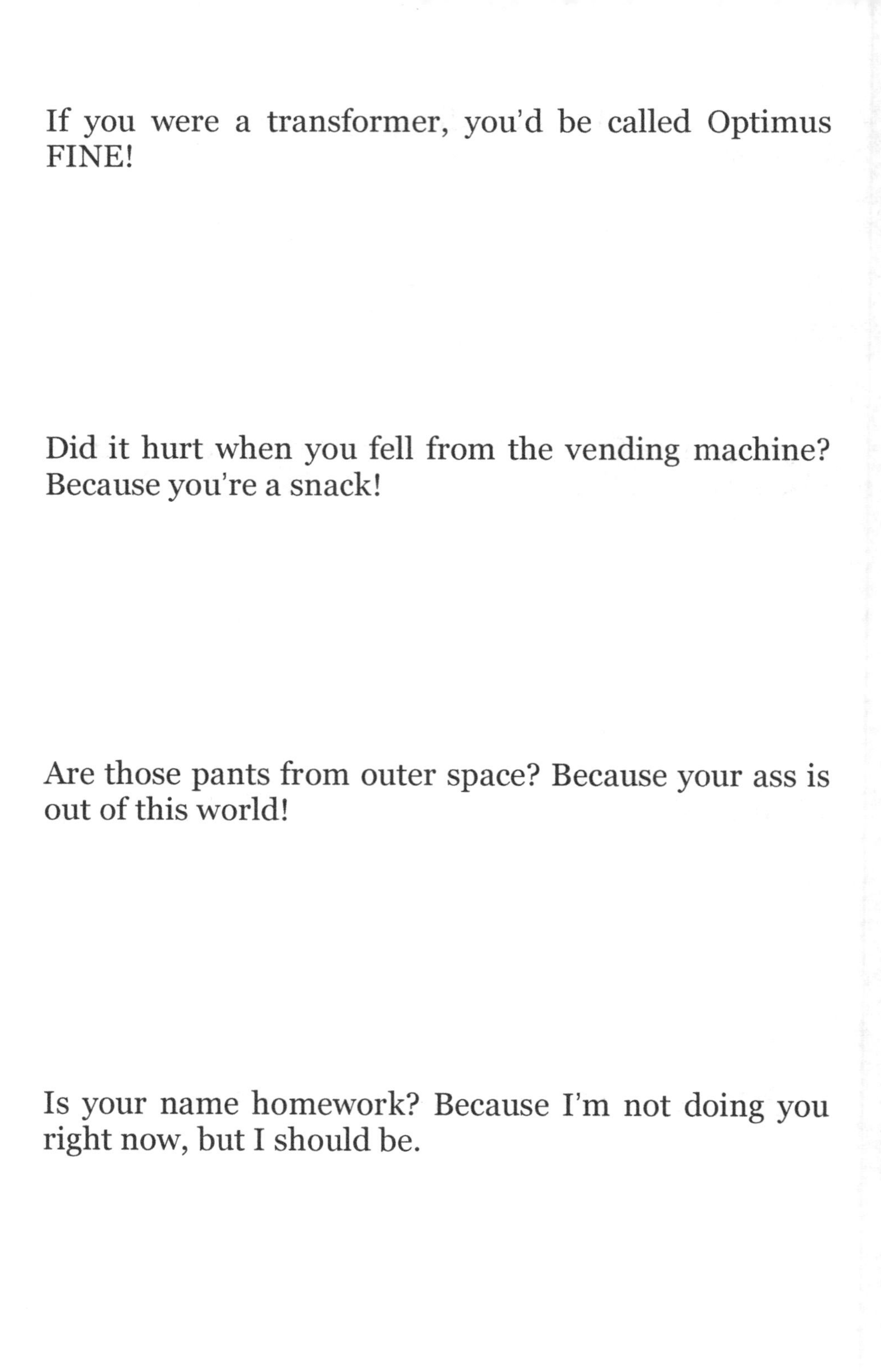

If you were a transformer, you'd be called Optimus FINE!

Did it hurt when you fell from the vending machine? Because you're a snack!

Are those pants from outer space? Because your ass is out of this world!

Is your name homework? Because I'm not doing you right now, but I should be.

If you were a vegetable, you'd be a cute-cumber!

Are you a chicken farmer? Because you sure know how to raise a cock!

There's a big sale in my bedroom right now. Clothes are 100% off!

Is there a keg in your pants? Because I want to tap that ass!

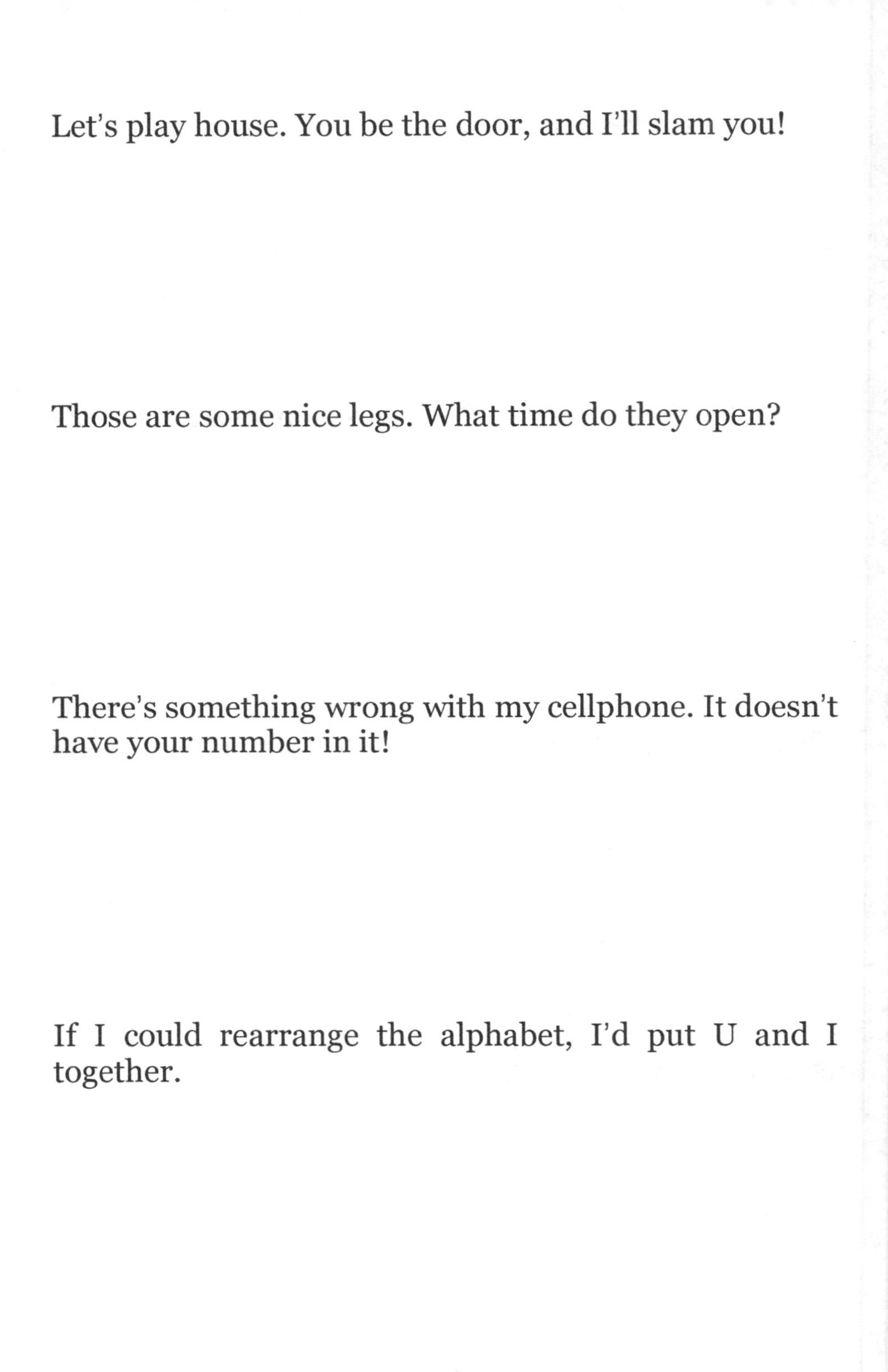

Let's play house. You be the door, and I'll slam you!

Those are some nice legs. What time do they open?

There's something wrong with my cellphone. It doesn't have your number in it!

If I could rearrange the alphabet, I'd put U and I together.

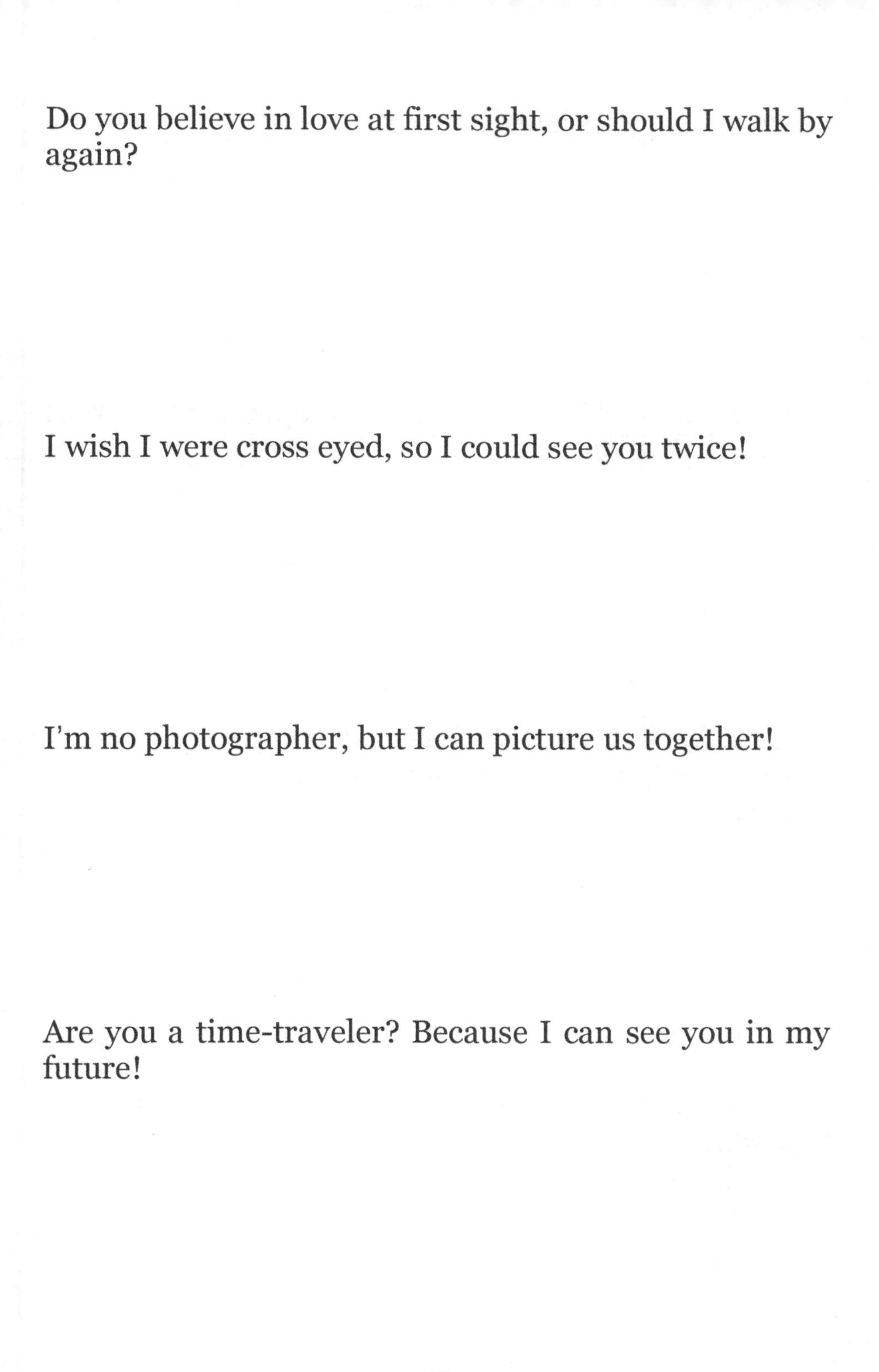

Do you believe in love at first sight, or should I walk by again?

I wish I were cross eyed, so I could see you twice!

I'm no photographer, but I can picture us together!

Are you a time-traveler? Because I can see you in my future!

My love for you is like diarrhea. I just can't hold it in!

Can you do telekinesis? Because you just made part of me move without touching it.

I don't think I want to have a baby just yet. But I wouldn't mind refreshing my baby-making technique with you.

Let's play carpenter. First let's get hammered, then I'll nail you!

Your smile is almost as big, warm, and lovely as my penis.

Are you a shark? Because I've got some swimmers you can swallow.

Do you like whales? Because we can go hump back at my place.

Are you an archaeologist? Because I've got a bone you can examine.

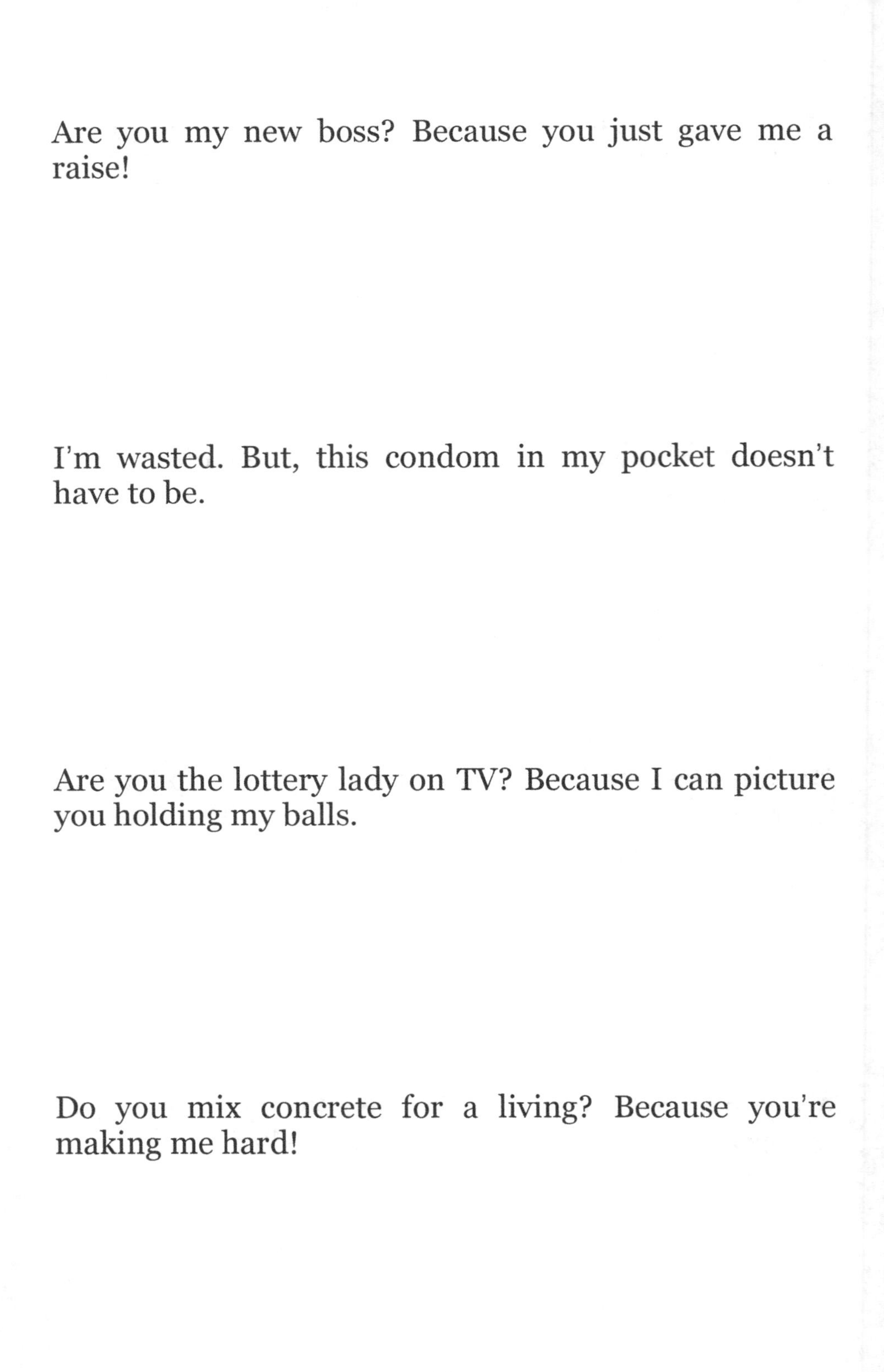

Are you my new boss? Because you just gave me a raise!

I'm wasted. But, this condom in my pocket doesn't have to be.

Are you the lottery lady on TV? Because I can picture you holding my balls.

Do you mix concrete for a living? Because you're making me hard!

That's a beautiful smile! It would look even better if it were all that you were wearing.

What's a nice girl like you doing in a dirty mind like mine?

Want to do a 68? You go down on me, and I'll owe you one!

Have you ever had an Australian kiss? It's like a French kiss, just down under...

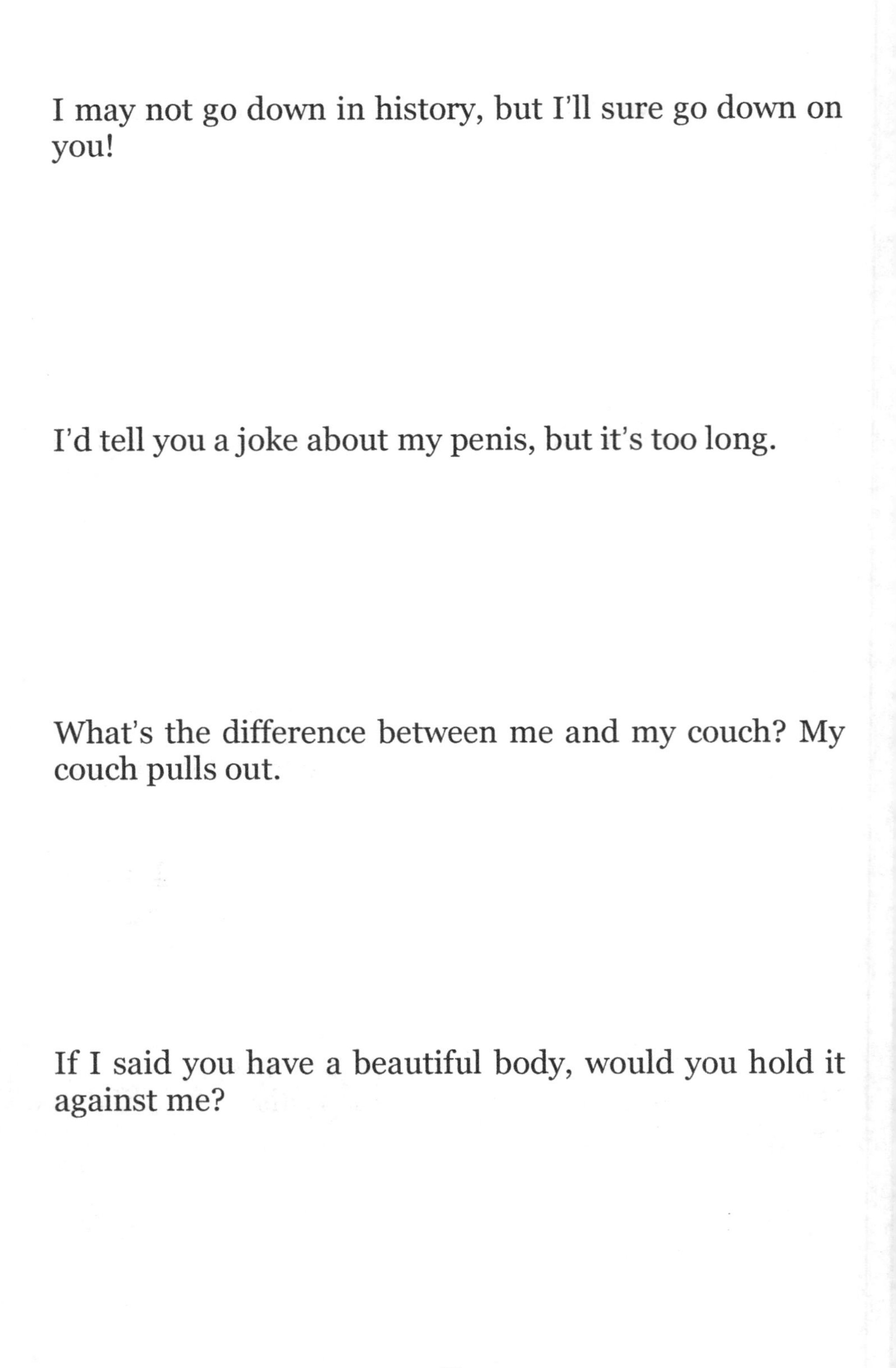

I may not go down in history, but I'll sure go down on you!

I'd tell you a joke about my penis, but it's too long.

What's the difference between me and my couch? My couch pulls out.

If I said you have a beautiful body, would you hold it against me?

Does my tongue taste funny to you?

What time do you get off? Can I watch?

How do you like your eggs? Poached, scrambled, or fertilized?

I'm a mind reader, and yes, I will sleep with you.

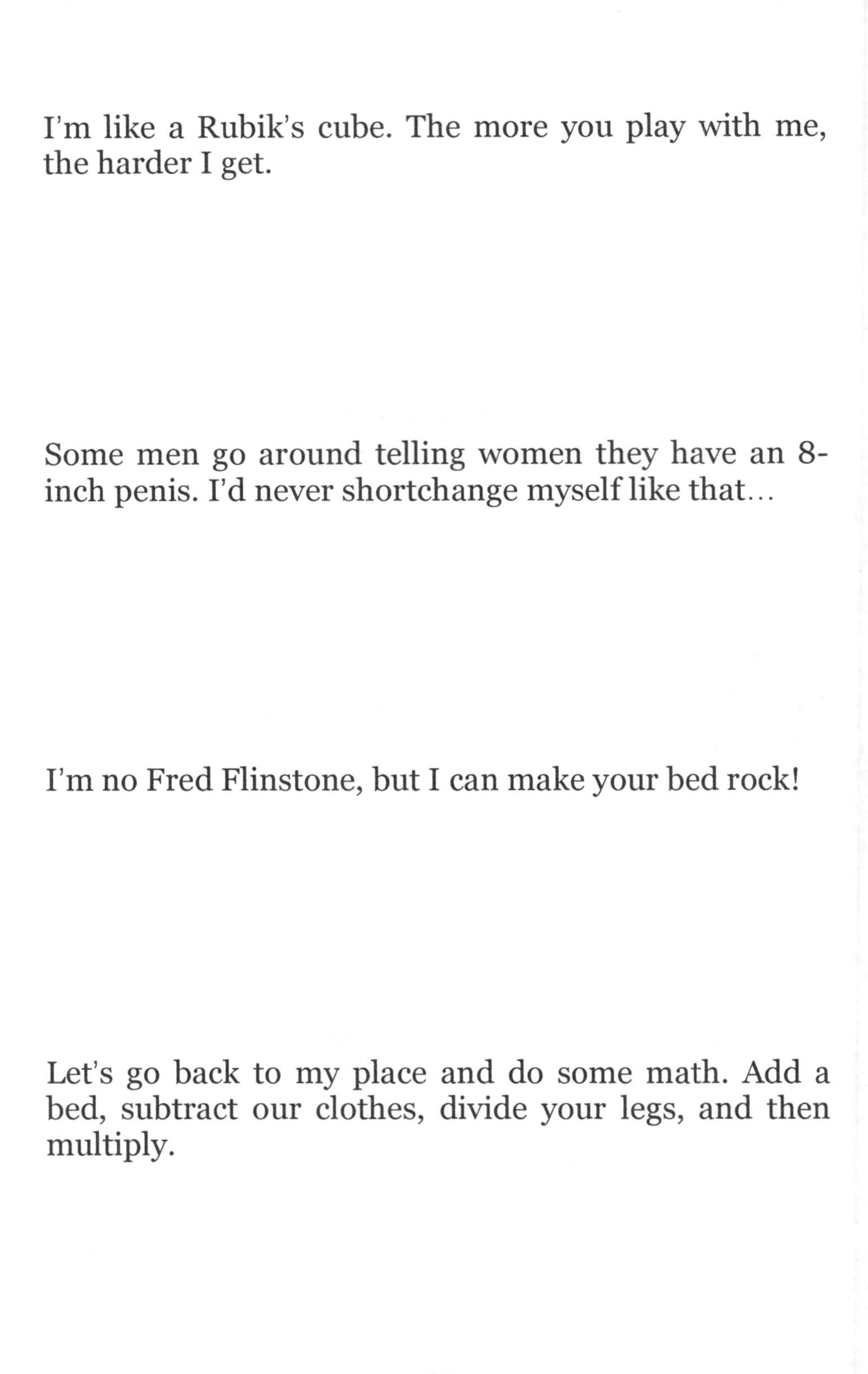

I'm like a Rubik's cube. The more you play with me, the harder I get.

Some men go around telling women they have an 8-inch penis. I'd never shortchange myself like that…

I'm no Fred Flinstone, but I can make your bed rock!

Let's go back to my place and do some math. Add a bed, subtract our clothes, divide your legs, and then multiply.

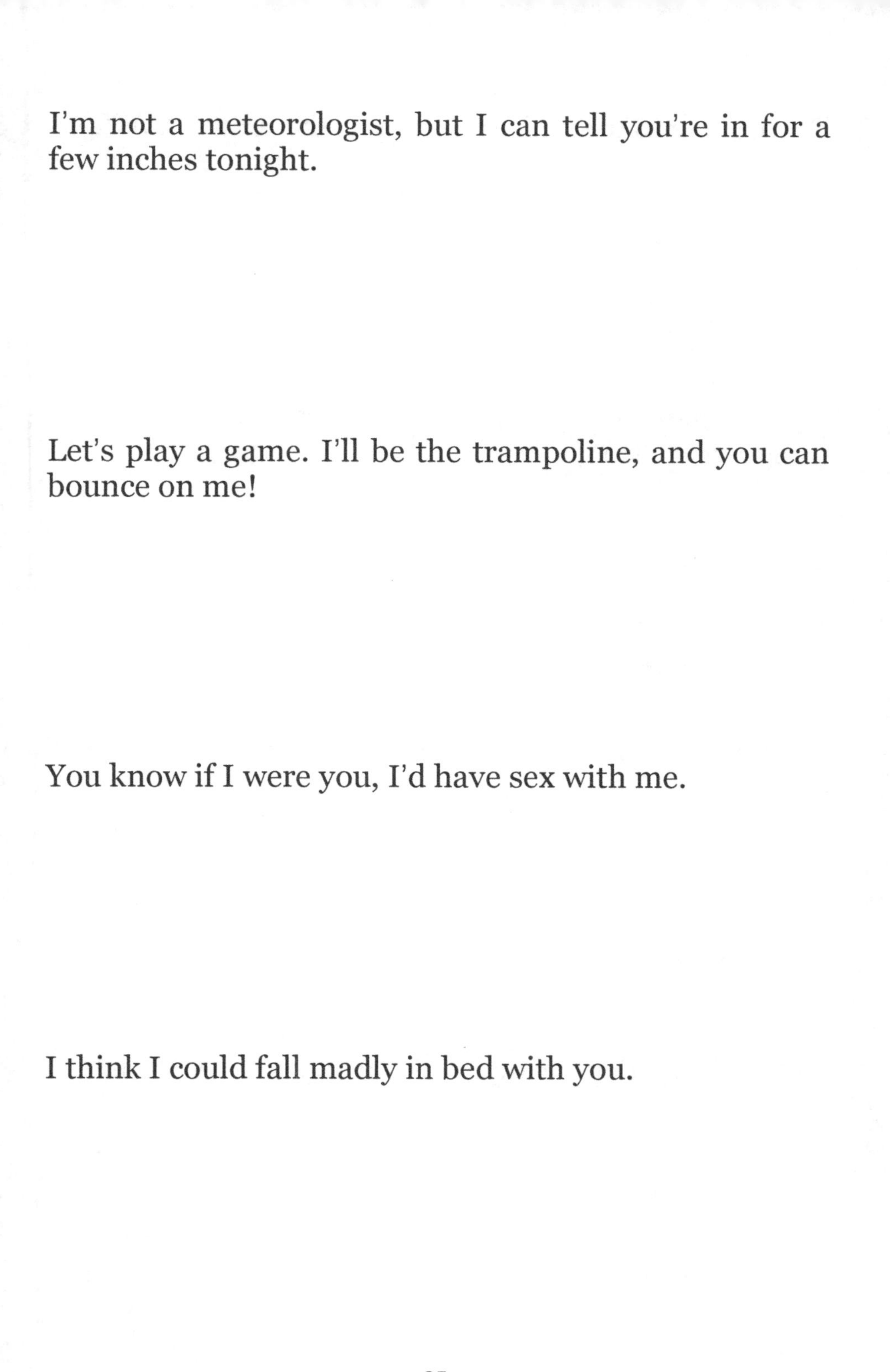

I'm not a meteorologist, but I can tell you're in for a few inches tonight.

Let's play a game. I'll be the trampoline, and you can bounce on me!

You know if I were you, I'd have sex with me.

I think I could fall madly in bed with you.

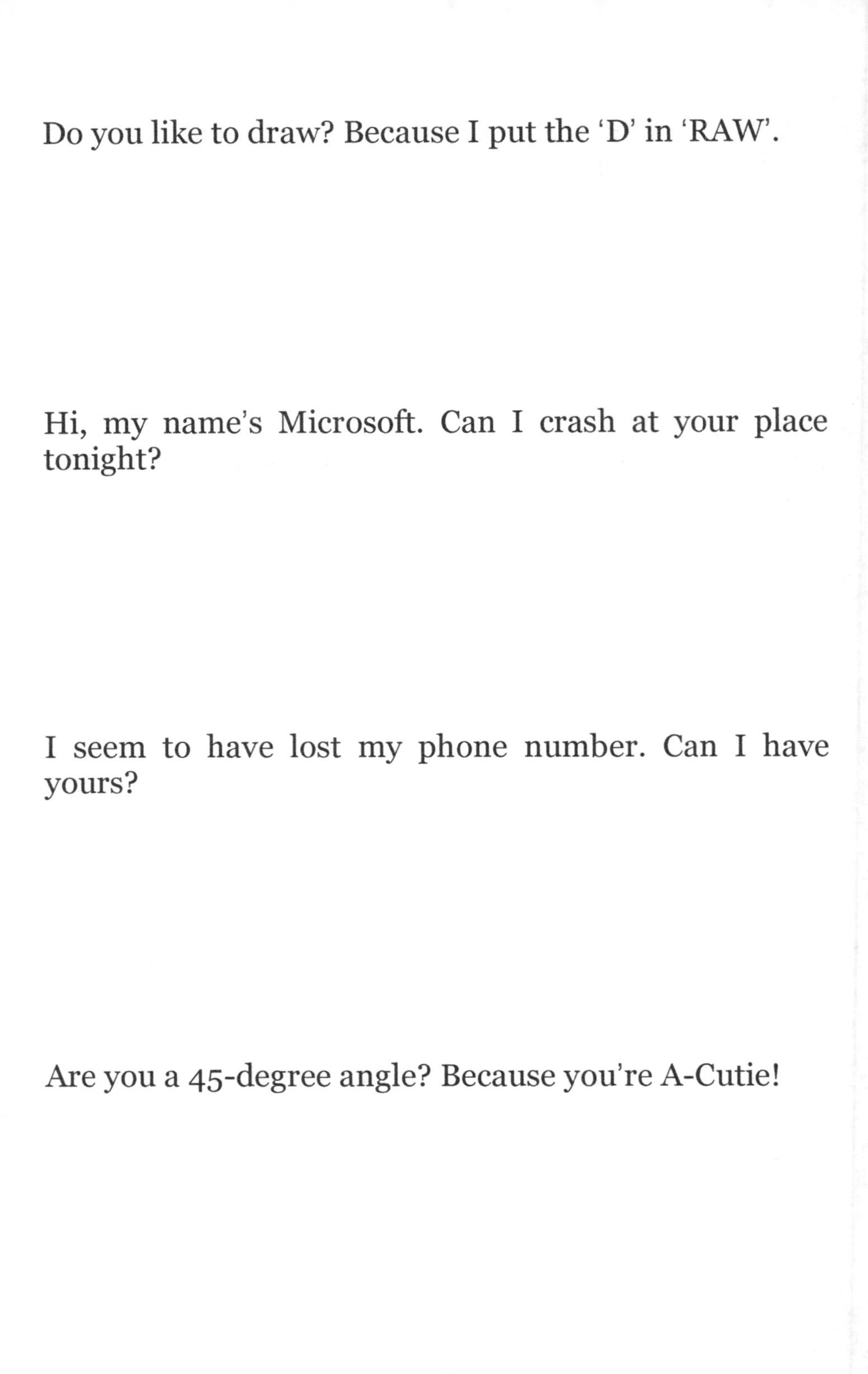

Do you like to draw? Because I put the 'D' in 'RAW'.

Hi, my name's Microsoft. Can I crash at your place tonight?

I seem to have lost my phone number. Can I have yours?

Are you a 45-degree angle? Because you're A-Cutie!

Do you have a name? Or can I call you mine?

Do you sell hotdogs? Because you really know how to make a wiener stand!

Hey, I'm bisexual. I'd like to BUY you a drink, and then get SEXUAL.

You know what I like in a girl? My penis.

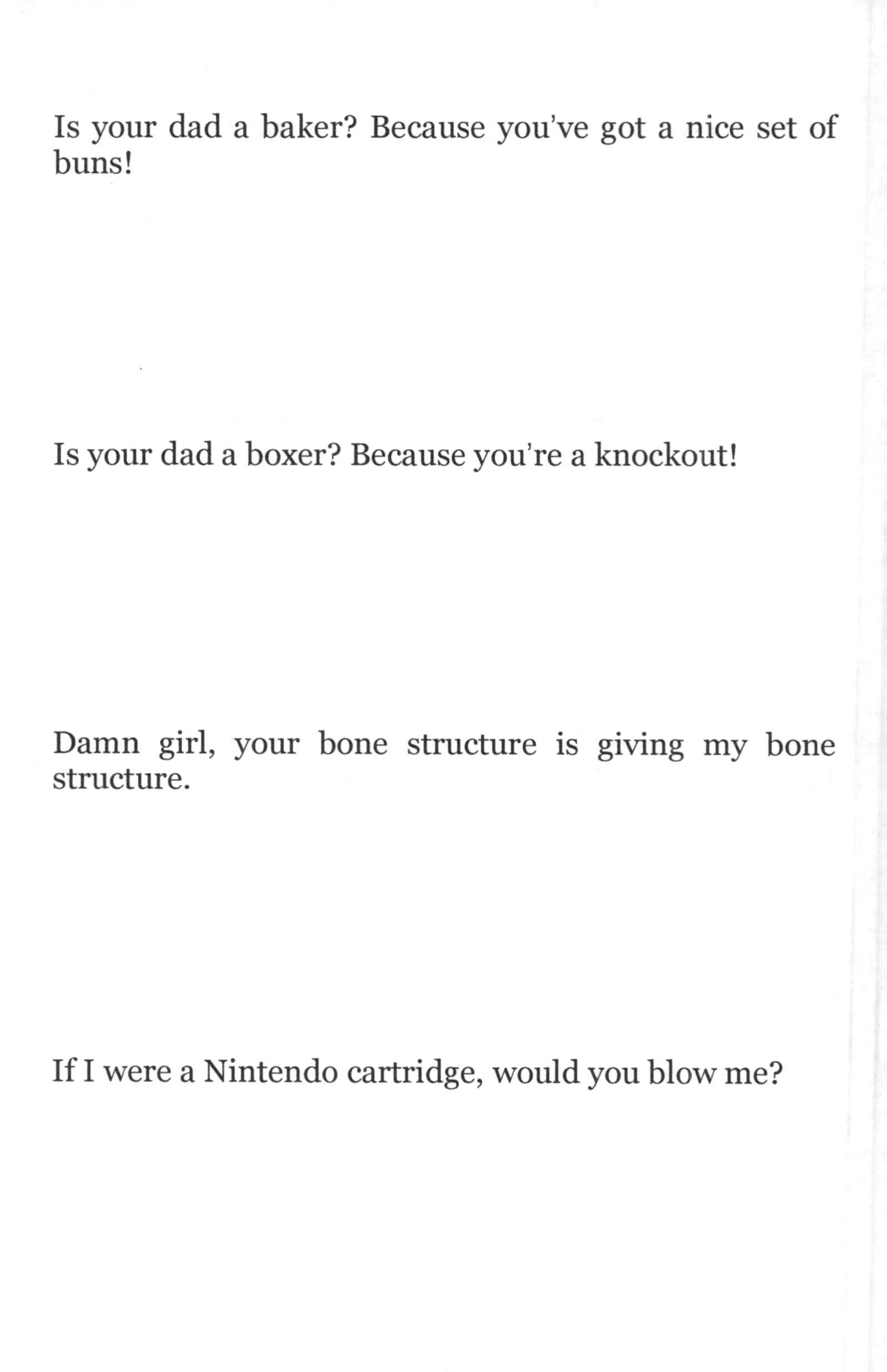

Is your dad a baker? Because you've got a nice set of buns!

Is your dad a boxer? Because you're a knockout!

Damn girl, your bone structure is giving my bone structure.

If I were a Nintendo cartridge, would you blow me?

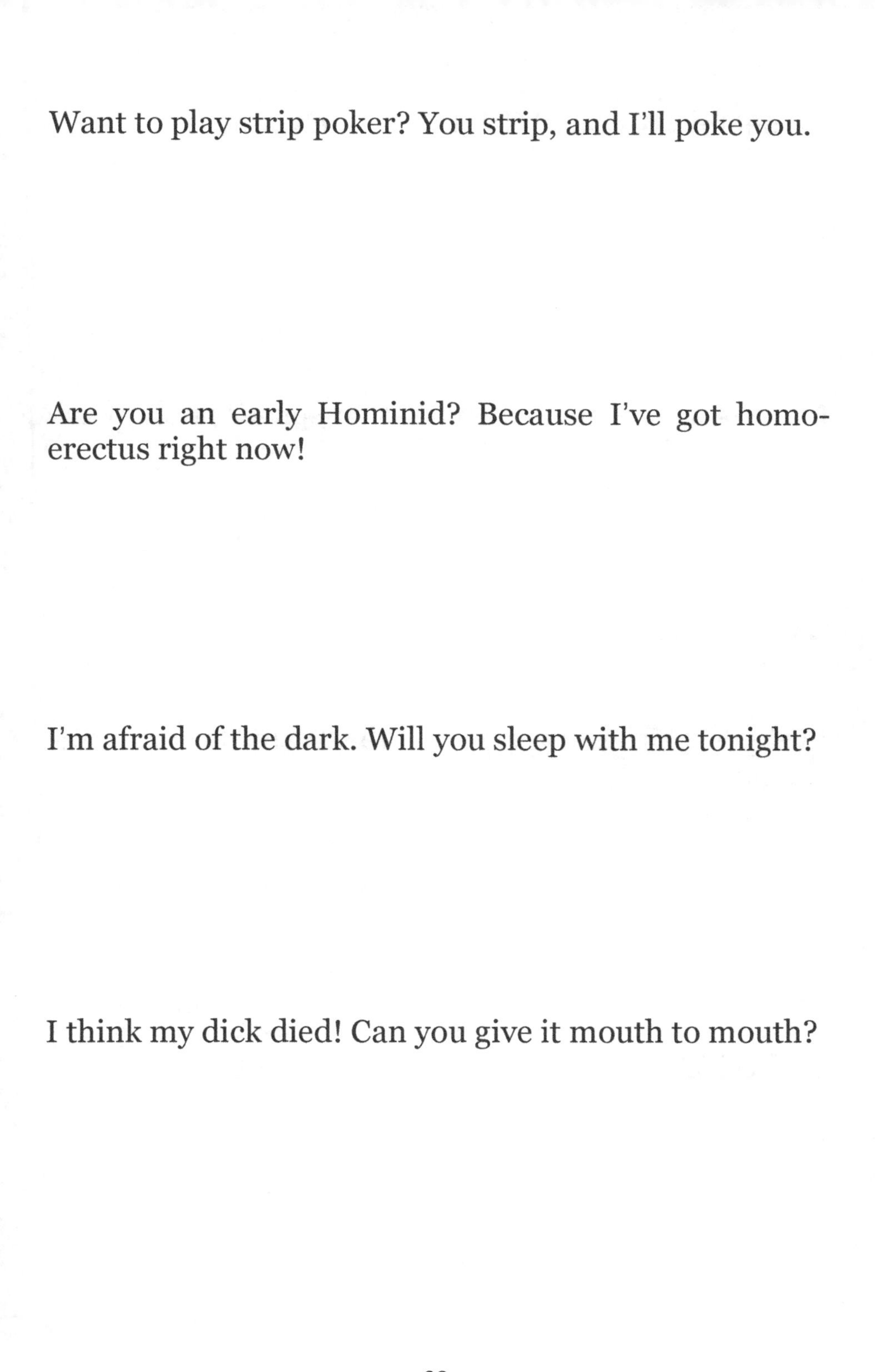

Want to play strip poker? You strip, and I'll poke you.

Are you an early Hominid? Because I've got homo-erectus right now!

I'm afraid of the dark. Will you sleep with me tonight?

I think my dick died! Can you give it mouth to mouth?

Oh no, my dick died! Can I bury it in your ass?

If I was a watermelon, would you spit or swallow my seeds?

I've got skittles in my mouth. Want to taste the rainbow?

So, besides me, what are you doing tonight?

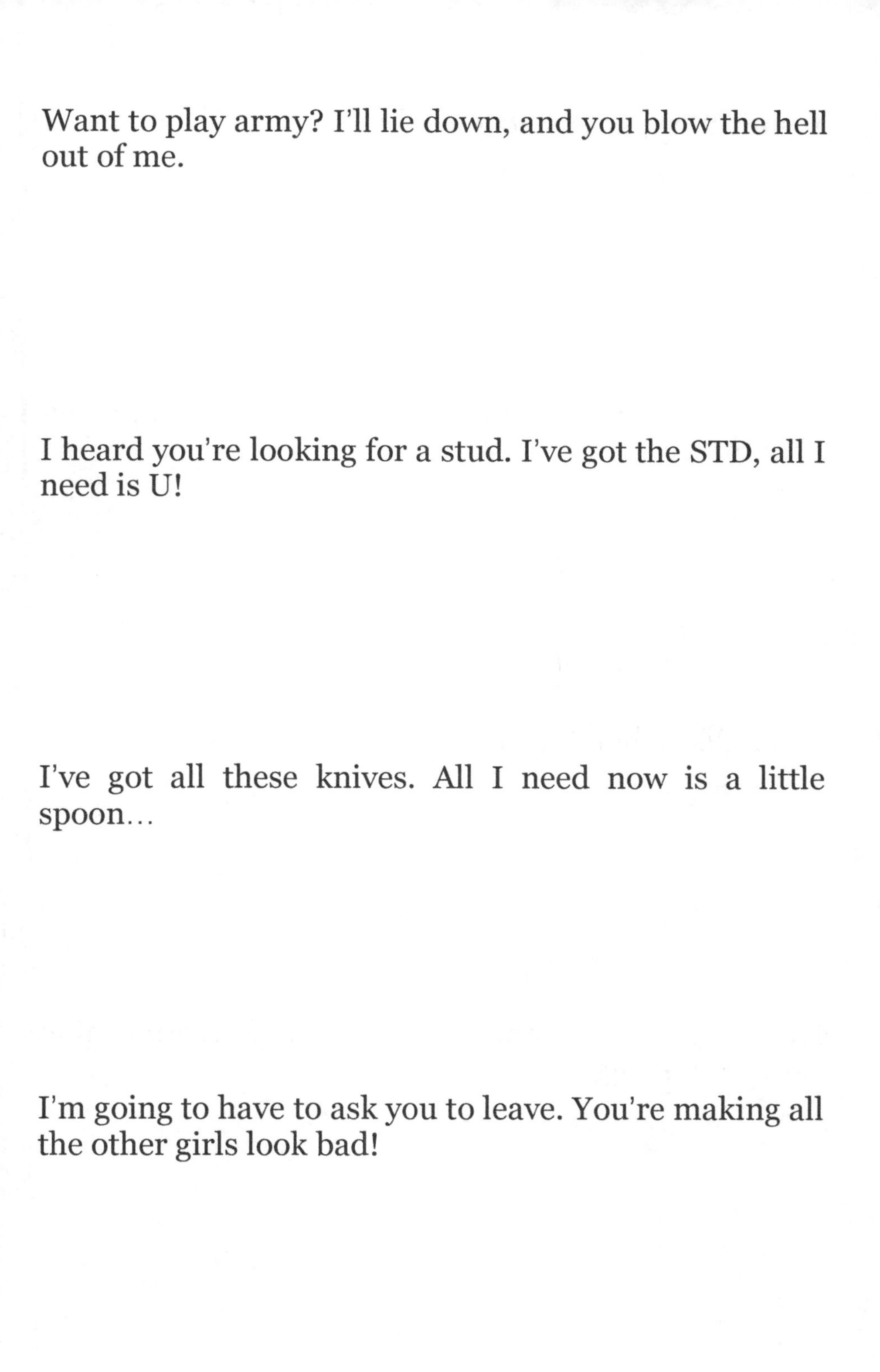

Want to play army? I'll lie down, and you blow the hell out of me.

I heard you're looking for a stud. I've got the STD, all I need is U!

I've got all these knives. All I need now is a little spoon...

I'm going to have to ask you to leave. You're making all the other girls look bad!

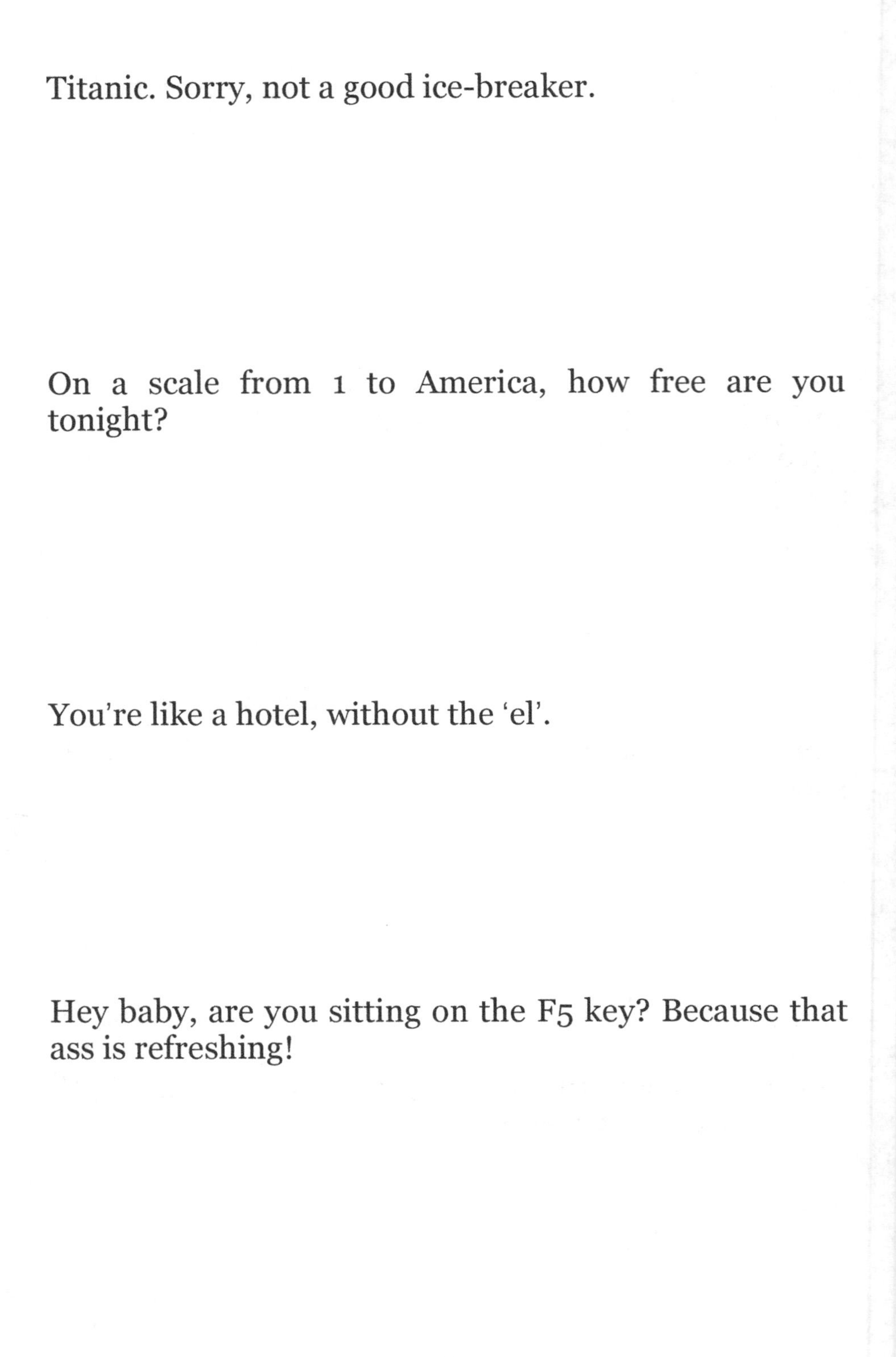

Titanic. Sorry, not a good ice-breaker.

On a scale from 1 to America, how free are you tonight?

You're like a hotel, without the 'el'.

Hey baby, are you sitting on the F5 key? Because that ass is refreshing!

Where have I seen you before? Oh yeah, in the dictionary next to the word 'GORGEOUS'!

You must be exhausted, because you've been running through my mind all day long!

I know you're busy, but can you add me to your to-do list?

If you were a library book, I'd check you out.

Your lips look lonely. Would they like to meet mine?

If looks could kill, you'd be a weapon of mass destruction.

If I were a cat, I'd spend all 9 lives with you.

Is it hot in here, or is it just you?

You're hot. I'm ugly. Let's make average babies!

Are you religious? Because you're the answer to all my prayers!

You're early! The Miss Universe contest isn't on until next week.

I'm looking for treasure. Can I take a look around your chest?

Don't let me be the one that got away!

Please tell your breasts to stop staring at my eyes.

So, what time do you have to be back in heaven?

Conclusion

Thanks again for choosing this book!

I hope you had fun reading and testing out these pickup lines for yourself. Hopefully some of them worked for you, and you didn't get slapped too many times along the way!

CPSIA information can be obtained
at www.ICGtesting.com
Printed in the USA
BVHW041345141020
591008BV00010B/841